Bull Sharks

by Deborah Nuzzolo

CAPSTONE PRESS
a capstone imprint

Pebble Plus is published by Capstone Press,
1710 Roe Crest Drive, North Mankato, Minnesota 56003
www.mycapstone.com

Library of Congress Cataloging-in-Publication Data
Names: Nuzzolo, Deborah, author.
Title: Bull sharks / by Deborah Nuzzolo.
Description: North Mankato, Minnesota : Capstone Press, [2017] | Series:
Pebble plus. All about sharks | Audience: Ages 4–8. | Audience: K to grade 3. |
Includes bibliographical references and index.
Identifiers: LCCN 2016051649 | ISBN 9781515770046 (library binding) |
ISBN 9781515770107 (pbk.) | ISBN 9781515770169 (ebook (pdf))
Subjects: LCSH: Bull shark—Juvenile literature. | CYAC: Sharks.
Classification: LCC QL638.95.C3 B35 2018 | DDC 597.3/4—dc23
LC record available at https://lccn.loc.gov/2016051649

Editorial Credits
Nikki Bruno Clapper, editor; Kayla Rossow, designer;
Kelly Garvin, media researcher; Gene Bentdahl, production specialist

Photo Credits
Brya n Clark, 19; Minden Pictures: Reinhard Dirscheri, 5, 11; National Geographic Creative/Brian J. Skerry, 21;
Newscom: Adrian Hepworth/NHPA/Photoshot, 7, Andre Seale/VWPics, 15; Science Source/Eye of Science,
13; Shutterstock: Fiona Ayerst, 9, Matt9122, 1, Rich Carey, 2, 24, Stefan Pircher, cover, Willyam Bradberry, 17, 23

Artistic elements
Shutterstock: Apostrophe, HorenkO, Magenta10

Note to Parents and Teachers

The All About Sharks set supports national curriculum standards for science related
to the characteristics and behavior of animals. This book describes and illustrates bull
sharks. The images support early readers in understanding the text. The repetition of
words and phrases helps early readers learn new words. This book also introduces early
readers to subject-specific vocabulary words, which are defined in the Glossary section.
Early readers may need assistance to read some words and to use the Table of Contents,
Glossary, Read More, Internet Sites, Critical Thinking Questions, and Index sections of
the book.

Printed in China.
004704

Table of Contents

A Bump and a Bite

A bull shark listens.

It races toward the sound

of a fish. The shark uses its

snout to bump the fish.

Then it bites the fish. Chomp!

Bull sharks live in warm seas.

They can also live in fresh water.

These waters include rivers

and lakes. Most sharks

cannot live in fresh water.

A Bull of a Fish

Bull sharks are heavy.
They weigh 200 to 500 pounds
(91 to 227 kilograms).
Their snouts are short
and wide like a bull's.

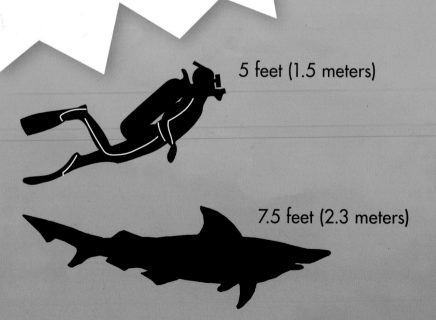

5 feet (1.5 meters)

7.5 feet (2.3 meters)

A bull shark's body is gray
on top and white underneath.
It has small eyes. The shark's
teeth have edges like saws.

A shark's skin has tiny scales called denticles. These scales make the skin feel like sandpaper.

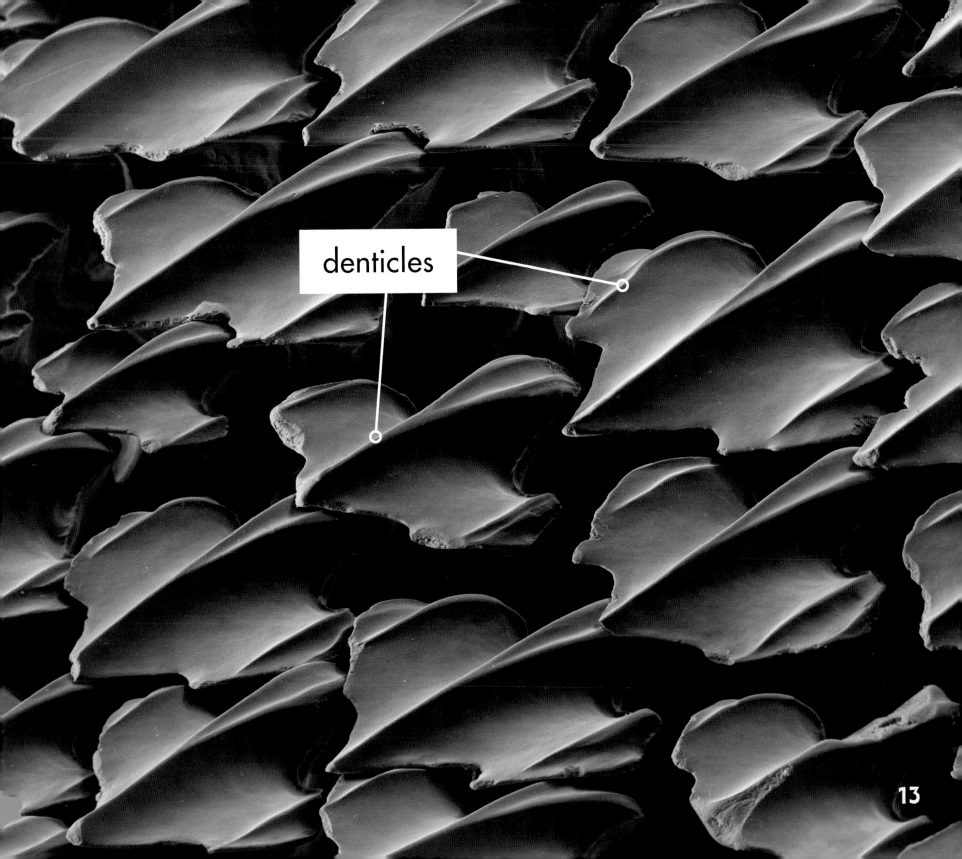

denticles

Hunting and Eating

Bull sharks eat almost

anything they can catch.

Their prey might be dolphins,

other fish, or even garbage.

The bull shark has the
strongest bite of all sharks.
Its jaws can crack
a sea turtle's shell!

Bull Shark Babies

Female bull sharks
give birth to 1 to 13 pups
at a time. The pups are about
2 feet (61 centimeters) long.

Bull shark pups grow slowly.
They live in shallow water.
This helps protect them from
bigger sharks. Bull sharks
live for about 16 years.

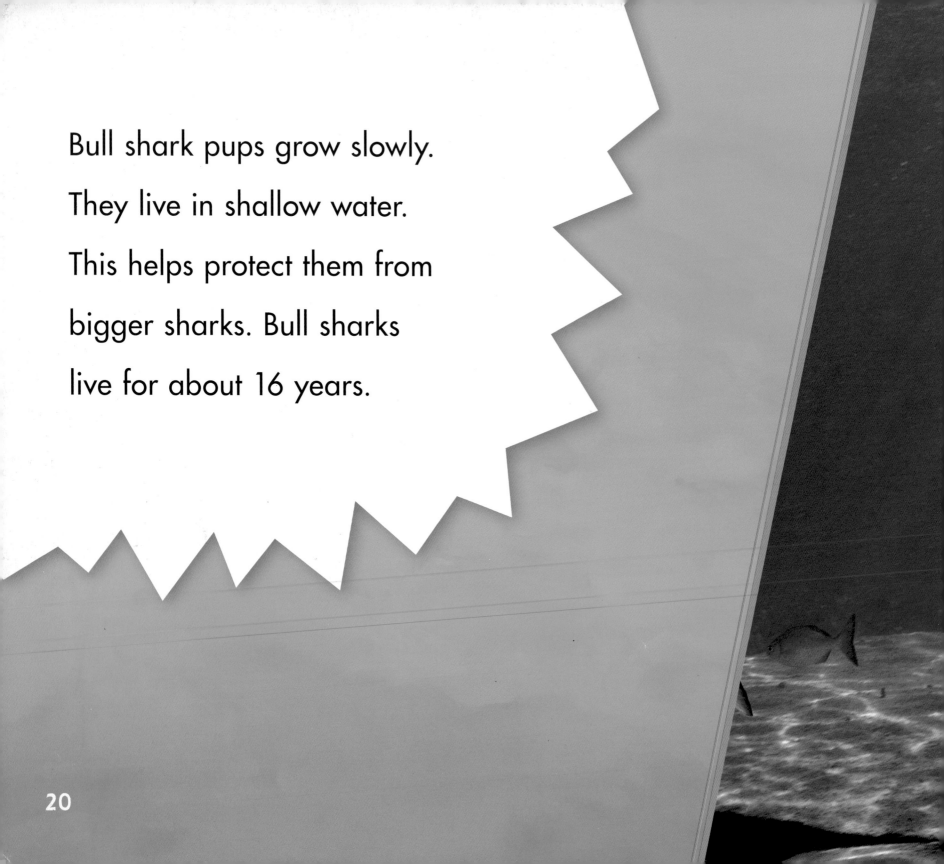

Glossary

denticle—a small, toothlike scale that covers a shark's skin

prey—an animal hunted by another animal for food

pup—a young shark

scale—one of many small, hard pieces of skin that covers an animal's body

shallow—not deep

snout—the long front part of an animal's head; it includes the nose, mouth, and jaws

Read More

Gagne, Tammy. *Sharks: Built for the Hunt.*
Predator Profiles. North Mankato, Minn., 2016.

Hansen, Grace. *Bull Sharks.* Sharks.
Minneapolis: Abdo Kids, 2016.

Meister, Cari. *Sharks.* Life Under the Sea.
Minneapolis: Jump!, 2014.

Internet Sites

FactHound offers a safe, fun way to find Internet sites related to this book. All of the sites on FactHound have been researched by our staff.

Here's all you do:

Visit *www.facthound.com*

Type in this code: 9781515770046

 Check out projects, games and lots more at
www.capstonekids.com

Critical Thinking Questions

1. What does a shark's skin feel like?

2. What is prey? How do bull sharks catch and eat their prey?

3. How are a bull shark's teeth different from human teeth? Why do you think they are different?

Index